THE LAST BEACON
SELECTED POEMS

BY
STEFANIE BENNETT

ACKNOWLEDGEMENTS

Some of the poems have been published in the following:

UFO Gigolo – Open Mouse Poetry – Westerly Magazine – First Refuge – The Foundation of Australian Literary Studies – Poems of Social Justice – Madness Muse Magazine – Alice Springs News – Beyond the Rainbow Literary Magazine – The Four Seasons (Anthology) – Every Writer's Resource – Reflections – Southerly Magazine – Shattered (Anthology) – Dissident Voice (A Radical Publication in the Struggle for Peace and Social Justice) – Haggard and Hello – Chicago Reader – Literary Responses to Asia – Dead Snakes – The Angelo European – Ink – Sweat and Tears – Kind of a Hurricane Press – The Galway Review – In Between Hangovers – Degenerative Literature – Plum Tree Tavern – Eskimo Pie – Illuminations Galerie France – I am Not a Silent Poet – Project Agent Orange – Verse Writes – Poetry Pacific – The Maleny And District Collective – Every Day Poems – Mad Swirl – The Best of Mad Swirl 2018 (Anthology) – Your One Phone Call – Orbit Net – Echonetdaily – Grey Sparrow Press – Ecord – Our Day's Encounter – The Australian – Lady Liberty Lit – Poetry Super - Highway – Pangolin Review – Poet Of The Week – Harbinger Asylum Magazine – Annual Holocaust – Remembrance Day 2018 Collective – Scars Publication – Lochraven Review – Rasputin – A Poetry Thread – Transcendent Zero Press – Ilya's Honey Quarterly – Haiku – Haiku Universe – Electronic Pamphleteer – Poetry 24, and others.

ABOUT THE AUTHOR

Stefanie Bennett has published 30 volumes of poetry. Over 50 years, she has acted as a publishing editor & tutored in The Institute of Modern languages (James Cook University).

Of mixed heritage (Irish/Italian/Paugussett-Shawnee), Stefanie was born in Townsville, North Queensland Australian in 1945.

Stefanie, an ex-blues singer and musician, has been fluent internationally in poetry online and in print journals. She has been nominated for the Best of the Net and The Pushcart.

Once again, a very large thankyou to those who have supported my work of words over the last few years, I thank you for the time you have given me.

TIME-LINE QUOTES

With certainty the poems ring truer than most shining in the poetic filaments of this country.

(Dimitris Tsaloumas)

One of the most original voices speaks through the great spirits of poetry and they through her.

(Judith Rodriguez)

The subject matter of the poems range widely. Stefanie Bennett is a skilled wordsmith.

(Michael Dugan)

If peace is in need of an advocate, then Bennett is a good one. May the hem of her skirts be stitched with hundreds of doves of raw silk.

(Keith Russell)

This book is dedicated to the Paugussett Indian Nation of Connecticut USA & the uniting of Arts Action for Peace, the ACF, the CFA along with many others who called for 'a nuclear free world' under the heading of ICAN - The International Campaign to Abolish Nuclear Weapons. I am proud & indebted to my lot for having won the 2017 Noble Peace Prize.

From 'Symphony for Heart and Stone': Stefanie
Bennett is one of Australia's most underrated
poets... despite what might be seen as one long
rebuff from the gatekeepers of Oz lit. Bennett wears
her heart on her sleeve and she shows in her latest
collection, an Australian/American publication that
she has lost none of her characteristic sharp edge,
keen eye and straight-talking voice.

(Tim Thorne)

Another woman, another world. Stefanie Bennett
does march, does walk, does slow, stop, move on in
her poems of often staccato erect rhythms
reinforced with the married notion of 'black' and
'boots'.

(Finola Moorhead)

Treating Bennett as a visionary poet the poems wear
two hats; one posited as a present lyricism - & the
second as a history of "Repel & Attract".

(Simon Eales)

'Stefanie Bennett writes poetry with a capital P. Not
for her the rueful ironies and domestic incidents that
make up so much of her contemporaries' work. She
insists on a bardic voice, an unapologetic moral
purpose and a communion with artists and true
poets wherever and whenever they may be found.'

(Penelope Nelson, Quadrant)

ALSO BY STEFANIE BENNETT

Shade
Poems from The Paddy-Wagon
Fronts
Madam Blackboots
The Medium
Tongues and Pinnacles
The Tenth Lady
Midnight Tulips
The Leaf, The Lion, The Lariat
Woman Of Straw
Three North Queensland Poets
The Hermit in Translation
The Vanishing
Blanks From The Other World
Muse From The Mountain
The Volatile Principle
The Pathfinder
Black Spring
The Sojourner
Resurgence: The Last Day
All The Yesterday's After

Performed Works:

Midnight Tulips: 'The Performance'
with the Sydney Seymour Group

The Novel:

'Stefan'

Cover Photo: By Tania Kavney

**Rear Photo: Stefanie Bennett
(By Tania Kavney)**

Contents   Page

Contents   Page

Stefanie Bennett

Contents

THE LAST DAY

After I have conquered some
of the world's ills in my fashion.
After I have climbed what's left
of the parasitical plot and attempted
                              to bring it down.
After the unwanted-wanted posters
have yellowed and curled
so that my name's been struck off
the records, the too human public records

and... I've greyed a little
and shrunk a lot,
and my hands have lost
                              their bitter cures
will you, once again, take me in –
take me in and not mind
this new stranger
as your lover of old?

Once I've been pensioned out – Yes!
I'm aware that it will happen.
Once it's known that what seemed
scholarly and spectacular was no more
                              than someone held
hostage by an everyday innocence.
Once I design ... the final line
and I've nothing left
to do, say, or display –

will you find it in you
to forgive the neglect
I shelved for you alone?

Will you
                    forget that –
I served but one light...
and that it was your light?
Will you mind... mind my return
    ... and keep this gypsy poet
    company?

I COULD NOT TELL YOU
for Anna Maria aged 10

You ask so many questions
I have to run, or hide
to keep up with you …

How often do
the great ones pass?
Is music
the only true language?
How come the raven
has blue and gold wings
in certain light?
Can a pebble
remember its origins?

Atlantis reflects itself
in your eyes.
Long-ago prophets
lend you their dreams...
their dying symbols,
and the witching hours
send you
moonbeam-candy
in the shape
of stars. You are
the sad harlequin
of the world's estate.

Your love is
out of time and place.
Yesterday, I found you
talking; talking to
a new-found
black rose.
Its thorns, they
turned silver
its leaves
- a softening red.

With your
invincible angel
as my witness
I should have told you
the rose
was dead; irreversibly dead ...

I could not. I could
not bring myself
to tell you that.

WATER DIARY

All the while the mullet leap
and splash and entice deep circles.
From my back door I watch
the kingfisher and crane
checking out the headlands.

One lone fisherman tends his net
with the agility born
of a race long gone. He whistles
and the wind carries a life-song
about the fig and weathered sandstone.

The day is laid out, winking like
millions of daystars
calling the comets in.
       A gull's wing
smacks the surface then glides
to a clump of reed and dead wood.

The mullet go on leaping.
I scribble into my water diary.
One day I will hand it to you as
a chronicle of home.
Like all mornings passed…

No sail's to be seen.
I write this
upon grey mudflats
and black moving sands.

NOW AND THEN

Those were the times, Nigel.
Bohemia at its god-forsaken best.
Chinese tea and gin chasers
down by the quay. We put the world
to order with a chant Buddhist-bell.

Those were the days. Sundays stoked
with Robert wanting realism and surrealism
all at once. And us, swallowing the lot
in the shallow rooms off Forsyth Street where
Dylan was king and Baez his queen.

We'd perfected the art of buffoonery.
Pete had an almost perfect
love affair with a third-hand printing press.
Carol spoke of dropping-in on Lesbos, while
Vicki made Nepal her marked Nirvana.

We dreamed our infantile dreams.
Crusaders of poets would rise up and
swat the mote from the earth's eye.
Clearly, we saw then in all innocence
what sets the mind to sobbing now.

Was it enough? To play at being tough?
The sacrificial years swept us down and under
a carpet of totally useless tomorrows.
You became a lay preacher. The others?
 I couldn't hazard a guess. And I? I go on

marking time. Occasionally word-knitting
a new bullet-proof …. vest.

THE SECONDING
for Christopher

I write for the boy,
the one with
grey eyes and future
not ascertained -
whose blood I bore
two generations back.

In retrospect I share
tomorrow through
multiples of his
dilemma adding
and subtracting
so the two become one.

What legacy in truth
may I leave other than
the engineering
of sound-wordings?
The portfolio
of metric kisses?

Yet, there is another seal
that goes beyond
the zone of kindred
kind, the surging
                    plasmic

                        spread

and a concept, natural as
the day of birthing.
Untouched. Intimate
as the night sky's
arrangement with
its cameo of powers.

This pre-recorded entity,
this invisible
seconding I give
to the boy:
The one with the auspicious
          grey eyes.

THE LETTER
Marina overview

Where did you learn to fill
your heart with sand-
to turn the midnight - blue
of your eyes
into circles of steel?

Whatever possessed you
to hold love's bullet
between your teeth?
All misdemeanours
cut just so deep. And-

whose portrait
                    was it
you carried?
What loss; what loss
tossed your vision
to the vanishing edge!

Through Prague's bleak winter
you howled, Tsvetayeva.
Your child - husband reported
'missing in action'. Your son
near dead of natural causes.

So... with the snowdrift upon you,
snow as crimson
as the totem of that
one rose
used as a fountain pen
... you wrote the world a letter.

Such high ideals. Blown
away in bits. You chanted:
Assassins! Assassins!
Fed ashes to pain
upon the unlit page.

It is all... Ghost-craft! Ghost craft!

Yet they will still ask,
                    rag doll
of the histories,
                    whatever possessed...?
Whose portrait...?

FIFE SONG FOR J.S. MANIFOLD

Memoirs do their own
inane conjuring's.
Hearing your voice
these many years past,
John Streeter, the persistent
brogue, the burlesque playback
- "You could tell he was styled
as a poet: He wore
those abominable
                   interchangeable hats!"

This ambiguous land's still
the Godhead ghosts get
fostered in. I listened
to a fife being played
along Sydney Street
- familiar notes. Yours -
and furbished back in the days
of rendezvous with
the Albert Hall,
before the bitter
embattlement of Crete.

Stepping sideways to avoid
the foot-traffic metropolis
you'd not realize,
the non-ideas of a new world
lionized in the unmaking,

I say you took
your leave just in time:
Thought engineers sell us
too posthumously, too cheap.

So, where land-bridge meets
both sea wall and shore
- stretching all the way out
to the heads, I wonder
… "How much ash
is you, concurring?"
Whistle deep now; bass booming!
A sonnet wings then sweeps
to the storm bird's … soaring.

MEMENTO: THE MOUNTAIN OF SUNS

'We are still living in Sabaoth lands'

The graticule
>   magnetizes
>   that Parthian dynasty.
And - the Arsacids*
>   once stoned with
>   the morphology of age
Rise, inexorably again,
>   to the old
>   humanistic order.*

The blacksmith's lame
>   enough - he walks
>   his orthopaedic curse.
>   The ferryman's
>   witnessing another pre-dawned
>   cult of the dead.
Women; children;
>   toss their loaded
>   dream-scream dice as
Colchis trembles*
>   Its blue acetylene ray
>   to the throb of a quartz lamp.

I wear the rose monocle
>   of reportage;
>   add my own salamandering:

Stark yellow …! Black …!
                My fingerprints smudged - denailed-
                        by muscovite wine.
No. Not even ascetic heroism
                can condone
                        a one-eyed troika mongering*
While all and sundry
                wear the branded
                        Goatskin lead-boot and cap.
There's three copecks worth
                of sound
                        forbidden your lips,
Enough to purchase
                the ingredients
                        for cabbage and mutton soup -

But, not the ballad
                of the ruins
                        in near forgotten Zvartnots*
- Or the malachite
                precision unearthed
                        within those Pushkin stanzas.

Here, at this moment
                most copious, I glimpse
                        the peninsula of Sevan*
Where stonemasons
                dug furiously
                        their foundations so that
A veritable lighthouse
                could be born
                        to shed gentle power

About the lands
            affectionately known
                as the 'mountains of suns'.

Who can forget, Armenia,
            your Moscow accent?
              your frock-coat
Cut in Ottoman style?
            your golden
              currency of cognac
Serving Japhetic philosophy*
            born of
              Noah's second sight?
The Hebrew prayer hands-
            Monks' tombs-
              And grand sea serpents?

Meanwhile, the iron staircase
            breathes a reticent
              Mythological track.
How gravity dropped
            three apples*
              in bold parenthesis
To three Esperanto
            citizens seeking
              harmony of civility.
The first parable told
            the tale; the second
              was for the one who listened;

And the third - helix of the ear-
            it marked
              the hermit who understood.

Prototype provincialism,
                    wry Ship of Peter,
        passes only
                    nameless graves.

The bleeding thornbush
                        keeps vigil
            to commissars
                    caught and set agape
ALL ALONG
                THE WATCH TOWER.

* Notes on the poem:

1. Arsaciads - ancient rulers
2. Humanistic order-Arshak & Shapur were
    legendary kings. Ref. is to Stalin's oppression
3. Colchis - other name for Caucasus
4. Troika - Russia three-man administration council
5. Zvartnots - locals live by the sundial amid the
    ruins where a rose is inscribed in stone.
6. Sevan - Armenian peninsula
7. Japhetic - relates that all pre-Indo-European
    languages of Europe belonged to a racial group
    named after Noah's other son.
8. Three apples = ancient Armenian fairy tale.

"All the days of the world
are written in this sand."

HELEN HORTON

THREE-DIMENSIONAL UNCLE

… Trying to explain you, crazy Alfie.
The spotted necktie
or cravat worn
at high noon:
Waxed moustache, turgid
aroma of cigar
and Crème de Menthe.
Negotiations and sign language
outside the school yard
of the Sacred Heart Academy.
You've carted
plump olives in a briefcase
for the Mother Superior
and the children.

Each pension day, peddling to and fro
to nowhere on
that 'Malvern Star' with
its bent wheel.
Pedantics from
the stationmaster:
"Impossible!
A return ticket to Calabria?"

Shell-shocked and twice christened
by both shores,
world prisoner,
one Easter

I took the gift… the sardine can
you said was
'full of arrows'
that flew
from the blind palms
of Saint Francis
promising never
to open it. I still haven't.

Half a lifetime later in
the 'nursing home',
you're adamantly stropping
the razor before
carving a jackboot
in the bedsheet.
"Yes!
The Orderly will
arrange a train ticket;
personal affects,
turn off
the rifle-fire
and leave
all the lights on. Crazy how
others are still trying
to explain you, Alfie.

THE SEARCH

Try to turn that thought
around…

The art
of waiting

for The Raintree
to flower...

The front porch
 rocker to

 move of its own
 accord,
          and you

God willing,
still in it.

LEVERTOV'S LADDER

…Leaving, she saw them eat
her words and
the left-over gravy

in that compromised tumbled-
down shack
        where
the hawkweed grows

but doesn't erase
the colour
of absence - or

the stony telling
there by
a turnstile gate

waving an even
darker reverie
aside…

THE SLOPE

Some never lose the thread.
A poet, a henchwoman
has need of a thread -
the toughest and most broad,
mark you, to lasso the golden goose.

I have
no such thread. Long ago
it abandoned me
    when the going got rough.

I tried to strike up a companionship
with missiles.
        With stars.
With rail speedsters.
        With storms…

They never
got off the ground.
My conversation became
the more tame.

Now? Time is spent in blind
fingered braille
counting dim golden eggs,
large as footballs, that fall
at my feet
      like hail.

HEARTS THAT DIE YOUNG

for Victoria Annamaria

I clutched the vision
of the magnolia
fine as pollen-
the coloured halo
of your hair.

Some hearts die young
without wilt or piety.
These are the ones
- Mater dulcissima,
I offer you now.

And this you'd known all along.
You took me walking
as a child, and through
child eyes you pointed
to the Imera's silken flowering.

Ever young - forever there…
You said. And as I fingered
blood oranges
by the seller's cart
and asked the whereabouts

of daystars and hermetic charts
your smile fell upon
the Madonie peaks:
Each answer the same. There was
no failed mystery in your language.

And now I clutch at visions; I've work
to do. Sometimes with
arrows that pierce
heart and paper. Sometimes with
rivers seeping, changing course.

But memory, you remind me,
is landscape enough;
scars - mended lines of living.
I raise mid-aged eyes
and the street of clouds

rests on a field of white magnolias
- ever there. Your final
word... Mater dulcissima.
It must be so!
Fine as pollen, as haloed hair.

THE DISCONTINUED EARTH

Beside the outdoor brazier
sprints
The Book of Psalms
and its 69
shades
of whipped up
winter wood.

All that's left is time's
wry labyrinth,
a star-spangled echo,
and a psychotic
ticket seller
        miming
'Red Sails
 In the Sunset'
        with
a whitewashed dove.

No stone remains
to be thrown…

LEAP-FROG: Fitzroy

You get the Kafka look-alikes!
You get the word eating strays
You get
desire's streetcar immobilised
in funeral grey.
Then? Well, there's
                    the Godhead
and an 'a' plus 'x'
nucleus quest
confronting
the Luddite theorem
that won't
                    give or get
the mythic handshake

of the Ferryman.

LANDSCAPE ORIENTATION

On the day the sun cried
an epicurean
semiquaver hung
above
the good red earth.
The cornflower-blue
horizon.
The jasmine's diminutive
austerity - and
the vanished
comings and goings
of providence …

Words, overheard - as
a crop
of ashes fell:
"It's the Bees Knees
of B-Grade movies
in toto
with re-routed

drone
escapees'
hijacked
        hearts".

Now, did you…
from behind
our cautionary
catchment
       see
what it is
I see?

PROBITAS

In the wintry
dimness
the ledger
crunched
its numbers:

The chairs offered
no sound -
their arms
        empty.

Just the legs
made of
Jacobean Oak
    strode
    through
    the foyer.

BOOKENDS

Dereliction and white noise
accompany the terse
glad bags of air
that our 21st century
has on offer.

The all-night pharmacy is run
by a smiling
"I don't take prisoners,
just bad- lander" geekazoids
whose euphoria
comes from
ghost-writing
medieval history
in fugitive French.
Dead set. My headset shuffles
the enforced 1812
Tchaikovsky overdraft…
Its liquid microbes!
Lost stars! And
the bleat
             of a carillon's
final round countenance.

TOLSTOY; Renunciation 2

Best forget why he's here
and from where he came.
If his step thundered
the blunt black bloodstone
of gunfire
amid the roses…

The Crimea wasn't a parking lot, then.
A September suburb
pummelled
by a double
or nothing
sequestrator.

Now, eavesdroppers
unerringly
find him
     defrocked,
         servile
and beating
tellable ploughshares
into words -

into a peace
that
shatters.

FOR ALL NUCLEAR SCIENTISTS:
The killing and the telling

Last night 'Terror' died.
It died, not as it had
lived in its own black death
but with the soft glow
of a green light about it.

I was cruel. I was kind…
I took from it the aches
and anguish of a life spent
battling the human elements.
I spelt trust as a four-letter word.'

Last night 'Terror' spoke. It spoke
in syllables as wide as the sky.
When faced with its own
ghosted-in image
the din cannot be described…

And I - perhaps with a little
too much of the Don Quixote
in me, wielding a rusty pen
instead of a sword
made the decision that

we kill for all reasons.
Some bad, some good.
And some out of pity.

I erased 'Terror' from the vocabulary
as if time's compass
had not ever
met this wretched one.
I do not know if the killing

will, in turn, intern me. There
was a green light
blazing about it.
Possibly that indicated
a pardon.

MILOSZ...the Caregiver

It was justice you saw that day, the tin
whistle and toy drum
left near the windowsill.
On side, the candelabra
wrestled with decay

as you'd done through many
a forgotten year
composed of
mild stupor and
Warsaw's tilled servitude.

If I could I'd draw a Sunscape margin
around the hospice hour,
add a peal
of winter bells
consoling to the ear...call come!

'Come! All you unseen freedom
revellers. Come play
in this
forensic nursery
of before
and after.'

CHEQUER

It wasn't perfect, we did not
go down
in flames
or fly
the cerebral kite
on shores
less foreign.

Drifting, interfused
with twists
of fallibility
and Gitanes
tasting like
              barometric
corn-syrup, we

read Ferlinghetti's
'City Lights'-
caught
the last bus
back

to specifics
that didn't add up
and an ending that
never was.

*"The most powerful presence
is absence"*

Dorothy Porter

A GENERAL TRUTH

The value of time
made tender
is when
two Sensei
Almond
flowers are
touched
with rain…

THE CAIRN

Refusing to float
they'll skip
across water
and dune-
this pyramid
family
first of
the line.

THE HURT

Way out west where
the prickly pear
grows
the salty sun
sits smack bang
in the middle
of
the road.

THE BRIEF

Sometimes - all
the moon
wants is
To let down
her hair
into
the river
of time.

HOME GROWN

The dust devil family
spins
like a top, kicks
like a mule and won't
ever
forsake
the past
for last.

SPACE ODYSSEY

Surrounded
by grey
days
you lose
when
love's
lost
in the wash.

STRUCTURE

It's not 'The Bracket
Creep' I worry
about but
the shadow's
eye
for an eye
deceit
of it.

PERCHANCE

The tortoise
waits
for
the post
to shift
of its
own
volition.

P. SALM 72

Since we've
bitten
the dust
our jaws
have grown
the most
improbable
prose garden

HEAT

With the egg nesting
in the attic
and the spotted dog
leashed
to an antonym,
any other
pursuit
seems trivial

RECONFIGURATION

The short-order
poet has
little to do
other than
peel away
the opaque
and
bury it deep.

GRACE

… I like boots,
worn down
a tad
and wearing
the land's
dusky leather
that
made
them.

CHECKPOINT

And there's
rain on
the rear-
view mirror
one
heartbeat
away
from here.

ASSERTION

What is it that
brings
the outside
in-
a good
book?
lousy
weather.

"When evening comes, once again the armies

of the uprooted march in my blood".

Nathan Zach

THE PERUVIAN JACKET

It's a little too old to wear now.
The seams? They're unravelled
like the most fastidious lovers do
... In the end. In the end.

Is it all that sentimental and undignified
to place so much importance upon
so many balls of wool; the hands
that worked that jacket to life?

Well, the wool was twelve-ply. The hands
arthritic but ever busy.
The garment didn't cost a cent except
for the attitude when I wear it.

Many cares and hurts have gone and come.
They've come and gone as these things do.
Nations have fought. Landscapes have changed
... the jacket! It's seen them through.

What's more: when it's gone, who'll replace it?
The inventor is with the angels now. These
days it's difficult to find someone who loves
and trades for free. She took the speciality
with her.

The jacket's been me, in spite of the age of it.
In spite of the scars and Man's damnable future.
I sport it as a trusty shield bred in the bones:
                    It warms my discontent
and remembers my aloneness.

MAY AND THE ROSES OVER

She's not dead to me. If she existed
as others she may never
have been born.

There's a table. Chair. Addresses scrawled
on envelopes; an abeyance columned,
squared black.

The usual. But too, that sunlight plays
about bay windows, across the ante-room floor
in much the same way it's done

on any early afternoon. Resonantly,
I say, "Mother's dead." What I mean is,
how unconvincing the ears sounds...

My sister, then. Teacher. It's closer.
The nouns. Life depends on them.
Be precise. Try the sounding again.

Another has it! My girl-child muses
over some vintage snapshot
of way-back-when.
          "Grandma's dead," she says.

Sound on that? No. I visualise
the empyrean mirror of us. Chant
assuredly, 'It is I. It is I.'

SHINE THE GULF for Tim

Because happenstance
likes
to play truant

the colour
of the smokehouse
is indigo...

Twirling much
as a prayer-wheel
does before

the river wild
sucks it on
back up

a full throated
February gullet
quieting

the Sandpiper.

INSOMNIA

Consider the ash
in its 3rd degree,
the partisan
         you've
made of me...

I succumbed, but
only when someone
had to lead the band
out over the walls

of the Infirmary.

Biographers, aspired
will fire
a line so slick,
was there

no more
to this
than
the music?

AFTER 'TRILICE' for Cesar Vallejo

No! I will not describe these trying times
in order to please
a referendum of lies
any child, with ease
can annunciate. Perception
is what you made it.

If distinction's a saving grace - say so!
If doubt crossed
your safe
hearthstone
question who invented
indifferent suburbs.

Objecting to a 'morbidity tax'
Libertarians - by decree -
have already
taken the streets
as hostage.
Gone are the days

when poets, under heaven's gaze,
saved cities.

CASUALTY

Distance... how far away
you've wandered
from the maladies
of attachment.

From the quiet room where
we read Kafka's tribulation,
my head resting
on your chest,

the clatter of pinecones
scudding the roof
and the wind
         at half-mast
soulfully singing.

Distance; a derivative
brought with it
an unbridled
dark steed

to infiltrate
         the yellow night-
         the red comet-
         the absentee-.

THE PACIFIST

Beyond reasonable doubt
there's an entrapment
the lesion
of the spirit
contorts to:

The abandoned echo
distinctly
        brine-dipped
hewn
into a judicial
stone kiss.

Perversity preys upon itself.
Humankind
is not kind,
        fevering
the white-washed hands
of faith's tactician

where hearts, hung
like Bedouin
relics,
are made
to be crushed.

EUREKA 2

Some days you are so far away from me
I cannot touch you with plea or prayer.
Through the complexities of sound I imagine
perfect poems, hexagrams, and stars that'd
wake the dead if I could but set them asunder.

What are you doing...Where are we going?
Was my shout too soft... My whisper too loud?
Friends of now, past and forever
- you historians of the heart, inventors
of truths
speak to me, of us; for God's sake, set it down!

Tell those, the ones who read you knowingly -
and those who, unknowingly, rip your lines apart -
how urgent is this need to reassess
the howl that hangs in the clotting air,
it's time we learned to temper that thunder.

There's no use in hoisting flags when
the dirge was sung so long ago. And my song, I fear,
is weakening also. I swear I stand on my own lost
echo and nothing, short of genocide
will send it back...

From the province of the Gun Runners,
where souls are swilled by high office Autocrats -
and ideals are auctioned off to foreign cash -
and the lame crawl one way only
                              I beat my drum
and call to you.

Where are we going? Where.

SOLTICE: for J.S. Harry

I've touched wood;
you were
the tallest
of trees
in such
a short paddock.

What's more,
the facsimile
of for -
ever's
still
sighted...

Right there,
near
the once
        named
endgame
base of it.

THE BROKEN BOUGH

Pick them up, the raw percentages
I've no longer any wish to carry.
These days I wrestle with the absolute.

Much is left over. The titan
impersonating Zeus' loss.
The white witch who sells

found fortunes at the half hour.
The sack-clothed singer
with the cracked voice and sad accordion.

New league missionaries. Bionic bards.
Assurance satirists. I'd bagged
the lot in some begotten springtime.

It was the evening my brother
returned from the war.
Quarter mooned - unlike himself

but with the sameness of quaint indolence.
Quieter than
our mother's grave. Speech therapy

would put a fix to that. It never did.
Years viced his silence
... lent me mine. I learned

communication's a game fit to kill,
squander, maim - or
tell untruths when amnesia wills.

Our sanatorium Sunday walks avoid
what it is that's left over.
In the distance I see them

impersonating posthumously those they'll
not become. Raw percentages
crying still to be lifted up.

KARMA-10

It was what the cat foretold:
Straying happens
but once in a while.
No homing device
was needed
to shout it back:
No rulings, no body-snatcher.

Of an accord best let be
cats return to

A cracked saucer-.
A sinking ship-.
If that's what
the tenth life
ordered.

PASSAGE - MOSCOW 1915

"I know the truth - give up all other truths!
No need for people anywhere on earth to struggle."

Marina Tsvetayeva

I've not destroyed myself although
they said I would.
I've run my race, but never crookedly.
The diversions, on occasion, were necessary.

And, I've not measured fate. Lady luck
had other plans.
Familiarity, fame - it's the same forgery
when you get down on all fours to look at it.

As for that plasmic boy, the one
who deals out icons
and the wearing lands of the senses,
I read him as best I could.

We lived separately. He, in his fine house
scattered with bronze eagles,
unicorn, and fire-wheels. I in my trench-coat,
total... convention less...

Mentor aside, the path was stony.
At every fork an ambush.
A reconciliation. Through the twin births
of opposites

I chose, always, what lay between.

After me comes
death in her doomed chariot.
I pause long enough
to kiss the living back to life.
I've learned destruction can be tender:

The process ongoing. The writing
of it seemingly natural.

THE DEVINE FEM

I've played down my stock of years
and kept the improvisation
for myself:

I designed the first heresiarch.
Mother to stone, feathering atmospheres,
my children hung as pendants;
the genetics of all.

I set the showground going.

The Muse had something to do with it.
The torch-swallower. The giantess
 of 'o' - and the gale that followed.

The tongue; it won't cease there.

MY GRANDFATHER'S VIOLIN

I can still hear my grandfather's violin.
He played as if he'd brought the whole
of Italy with him...

He'd been a barrow-boy; he'd sold fruit
and flowers outside the concert hall
of Naples. He'd seen and known Caruso's last
performance from the back row.

That concert cost him thirty barrow loads
and nine days of hard selling.
"I'd do it again," he'd say. "There are
many apples but too few phenomena."

I can still hear my grandfather's violin,
hauntingly beautiful, drifting upwards
like a prayer - like water trickling
about the flagstones in the back garden.

I see the old photographs hung near the stairwell.
The pin-stripe suit. The classic spats and hat
that lent 'a touch of class' but more than that.
His kind of tenacity shone on through.

He went as he'd lived. Glib and humorous.
His policy? Things are what you make them.
He died comfortably off. It started
with a barrow full of fruit and flowers.

The violin? It held it all together.

SCHILLER'S 'ODE TO JOY'

The tribe is not lost...
Replacements will come,
you'll see.

The bloody axes
                    will come.
The sonic blowpipe
                    will come.
And later 'the book'
                    will come
wheeling in
              its missionaries.

              All will come -
as past becomes. Everything
reserves some right to glory.

The tribe is not lost.
Its too human face
has simply
              fallen.

DOWSING

One blade of grass
will weather all seasons,
trawl spider threads
through the chimera wound
as D-day approaches.

Listen. Do you hear the crib
shrieking empty
in the holster
of the wind? That's
convergence!

One blade of grass -
                    flexible,
coverts the key
to antiquity
and stays
the discus thrower.

Not of this era, passers-by mistake
transparency for rubble.

BATONS AND BOONDOCKS

Why am I dreaming
of young grenadiers
and the night's
mawkish militancy!

A carnation, unwieldy bowed,
receding
in a row
of saltbush

that didn't turn
true-blue
        but peaked,
lacquered
thin as

an oppressed mortal's
herring-
bone
shroud and

the stoked-up
ricochet
of attrition
on the run!

Must be Faust's off-siders
doing the rounds.

MINIATURE

As lady-day
begins
to fade,
the yellow
bird
voices freedom.

In the blink
of an eye
        - working
over-time -,
she holds up
the sky

and its Saviour.

TIPSTER

On nights of the full moon
I batten
down the hatch
for who knows what city-slickers
will tally up to.

All and sundry's fumigated,
especially the wicker chair
belching collywobbles and
covered in hoar frost
...the lair where

an enthused meteor squats
and resumes his Promethean
shock-jock tale
of devil's dust
gone loco.

Beware the pith and marrow,
he intones.
It's 'sucking eggs'
that make
wise counsel.

BETRAYAL

Clocks. There are too many clocks.
There are too few many homo sapiens
who do not aspire to clocks.

See the mouse run. It is the machinist.
It attends the clock arms.
In any event it'll corrode with the battery.

Attention! The clock has gone sour.
She spat out her spring. Disrupted
the schedule of trains and the iron bird also.

What to do when the clock revolts?
When the clock family, a billion-fold,
climb down from the wall and leave it...

We know what we'll do. A concentration camp
for clocks in peacetime's a bore.
Say, what else is our military for?

FLIGHT

With the infinity of rivers flowing
through my veins
a miniature sphinx becomes my body.
Day is married by my left hand
and the estuary of the heart
is calm; full.

Any postcard I write is empty.
What I mean to say
                is speech
welcomes the superficial;
we attach
too much importance
to sound.

Quiet brings forth her disciples
- Sphinx and Ghost -
who've slept centuries
between the condors,
etching out
the subsidiaries of space.

PREPONDERANCE

He said, 'I lend you love'
which meant - lease;
the aftertaste
of lips
dispersed
on spent tourmaline.

The attaché of indifference
doesn't come
to terms
with chancery;
doesn't see
the meteor fall

or how she aggregates
the delicate
architecture of a leaf...

CONVEX AND THE BODY POLITIC

After all the faux pas the living polaris
goes on extrapolating
the undergrowth
of bare-arsed wars
denser than a hare's breath,
lighter than
captivity's raw innocence.

We wait. We wait for the thaw in the heart
of another derelict season
but the elements,
like run-away children,
outwit us.
How long it is since the cricket
brought good tidings!

What I need now is the hint of laughter
and my mother's face
framed by the fireside.
She'd know
what to do about
impoverishment;
the evil eye that's

catapulting over
the moon's rock-of-ages.
'Nettle soup
        scalds
a despot's whim' and
stark truism is the stench
        that lingers...
        deafens.

STRATUM

An enemy is nothing to sneeze at:
Often his eau-de-Cologne's
all embracing;
the fraudulent grin hinged
upon tit-for-tat circumspection.

If you should sight him
parley on
that I am well endowed
and cluelessly
abandoned.

Figuratively I understand
just how faithful he is.

RILKE'S DESK: A POSTSCRIPT

The day, like no other,
wipes its brow
on the petrified sun
and dreams
the autonomy
of an ilex tree
ascending Jacob's Ladder.

For now, you have
inherited the pinch of
a prodigal hour,
          grown
the starling's plumage
in variable shades
of tumultuous dust.

Be gratuitous. Don't
scramble
      the cornucopia!
With wind-swept hands
we draft
the ledger.

BURDEN

He's a mite sore, tired
and querulous
from diving through
atmospheric
fish-net stockings
sucked up
the nebular sprout
when the land
froze dry
and the turntable
tipped headlong...

How grave is gravity's
decline!

It's not
      hearsay -
the moon's
got a bad back.

OMEN AND AUTOCUE

The moment they wake up
and the ransom's paid
from the cup of antithesis,
there'll be
arm wrestling, slogans,
a fixed stare
fused
to the evening papers.

Someone said that on Civvy street
the coroner's couch
was seen 'dancing in the dark'
and, there were prayer-shawls,
coupons, and miscellaneous
flagstaff's waving
iron butterflies
as noxious as distemper.

Still, the high-definition revolt's
too debonair
for the retired post-mistress
- AKA, Job's wife
who aims

a sling
-shot
at the Pearly Gates

and dresses the wound
with salt.

TALLY

They stepped lightly about
the indelible divide
- past the voiceless harp
and into the parlour of days

where a drift of incense
encircled the hat-rack
and the begonia,
grim and proper,
                         dropped
its truce.

None came out.
None stayed.

ARRIVAL

They are wary. A nobody's in transit
scantily clad, but his biceps
bulge and tweak of royal favour.

Risen from mortal metaphor,
he crosses the boulevard
                              that isn't there,
sips permafrost through a glass straw.

The bleak foothills fracture parallel
after-shocks, and mastic cloud
hails linchpins.

Only when he unfolds his swag
to lie down with the lamb
will the town-crier quietly assert
                    - 'this one's Zarathustra'.

DOVETAILING SUPER-AESOP

"This is not the Arcady Realm,"
said the pauper
to the priest, who rolled
his own tobacco weed
and borrowed
lightning's ember.

The 'dramatis puppetry'
let out
a full throated
metaphoric
stupefacient
bass-release

and the barbarian
in the bathtub
phoned 'Home',
collect.

EPILOGUE for Dan Pagis

There is no train.
There is no station.
The stopping point's
beyond recall...

Yet, there was a house.
A lamp. A window
through which
the forest
        entered
following
a sky-rail - and
tomorrow's
apocalyptic
swan song.

THE MASK

She likes peach-tree branches
that touch the earth;
topaz wrist bands
and 'kicking over
the traces'
of what
a vanquished
homeland means.

Aged all of three
knickerbocker
summers,
the Mestizo
girl-child
will
    or
won't
go far on
the shortest
    of roads.

SEIZURE

In my father's house
 a deceptive land,
 an impulse
 waxed lyric

while unencumbered
the axe-head
and wood block lay
seen only
        from
the bi-fold window.

There - time stepped through
the filaments'
grasping squall
telling all
how I am now
        twice as able
as once was Cain.

MULTIPLICATION

What shall we do with the wounds
        We are imprisoning the thorns
What shall we do with the thorns
        We must save them for the final dictator
What shall we do with the final dictator
        We will make of him a puppet-master
What shall we do with the puppet-master
        We'll tell him how beautiful he is
What shall we do with beauty like this
        We can teach how reflections lie
What shall we do with such reflection
        Ah! Bandage the product and shelve it
What shall we do with the shelved product
        ... Just feed it to the thorns

As they multiply. Multiply.

SPELL-CRAFT

Forget the shale and thorn-tree;
the boulder
just lay there
            static
between the okra and
the eggplant
            until
besotted smoke plumes
and an eruption
scuttled
            around the bend like
a leap-year's
            psychosis.

Hi- Ho...!
            Sisyphus.
            The worst

            is over.

PARALLEL DISSERTATION

Raise the tempo. The flag
that waves back.
The water-melon-man's rumba
and Stravinsky's Rites of Spring.

Picture this when I have mellowed
... love, and the origami's
coiled and cold,
as time goes marching

leeward and the urn's turbulence
unfolds
      a renewable
lease of space.

CIRCUMFERENCE

We are already vanishing. The curse of
it all cries benevolently.
Circumstances stand
and remind us how love has
cut us, cut us clean.

I have picked you a bunch of wild strawberries.
Take them with you
when you leave. Don't turn to thank me,
I am smiling,
believe that. Believe that.

You must not ask me questions, an answer
just won't come. My tongue
is still. I am lost
in my own precise solitude; wait
for the sound of retreating footsteps.

There'll be no written word. I promise I have
time only to reconcile, conceive.
It will occupy my life-form,
replace the latch
and our worn heart's door.

Forget the handshake. Remove your fingertips
from my sodden sleeve.
My laundry is as unkempt
                              as I am:
Assuredly, I'll do what I please.
Can you believe that?

Believe that my bent head is a courtesy.
Believe that I am way past assuming.
Believe that a fruit-picker
has her obligations;
I am tending a torn patch on my knees.

We are already vanishing. Believe that!
Believe with the same candour
you show in believing me.

"Thank goodness somebody thinks poems are forever. What you say of Tsvetayeva may as well apply to you" ...

Judith Wright

"We love your work. Congrats & welcome aboard!"

Poetry Pacific, Vancouver